MW01096560

DATE DUE

SEP 23 '85			

83-934

Greenhaven World History Program

GENERAL EDITORS

Malcolm Yapp
Margaret Killingray
Edmund O'Connor

Cover design by Gary Rees

ISBN 0-89908-010-3 Paper Edition
ISBN 0-89908-035-9 Library Edition

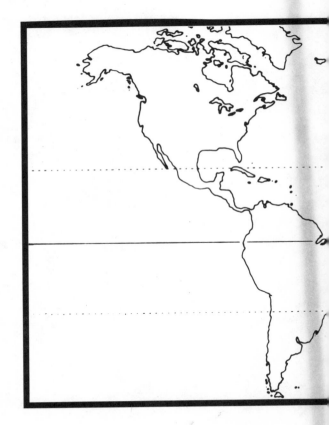

First published in Great Britain 1979 by
GEORGE G. HARRAP & CO. LTD
© George G. Harrap & Co. Ltd. 1979

ASOKA AND INDIAN CIVILIZATION

by H.A. Kanitkar
and Hemant Kanitkar

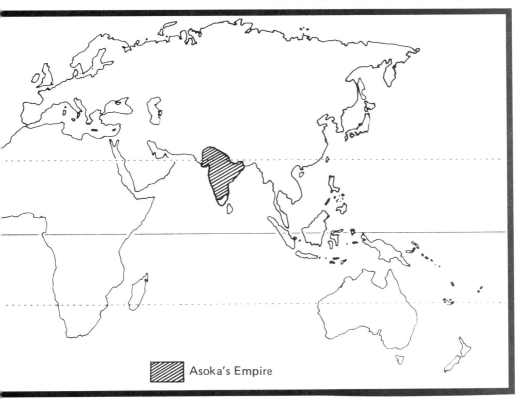

Asoka's Empire

Greenhaven Press, Inc.

577 SHOREVIEW PARK ROAD
ST. PAUL, MN 55112

Each great civilization has its own distinct way of life, which we can see through its political, economic, social and religious systems. In this booklet we shall look at the way of life of traditional India during the lifetime of one of its greatest kings, Asoka, who ruled from about 272 until about 236 BC.

Asoka was the third ruler of the Mauryan dynasty, founded by his grandfather Chandragupta (c.324 – 302 BC). The power of the Mauryans was based upon the Ganges-Jumna valley, in northern India. Because of its wealth this area was the centre of power for all the great Indian empires. The Mauryans were the first to build an empire which covered the greater part of India. We shall look first at this empire and then consider the social and religious systems which existed in India.

Two of the world's great religions began in India — Hinduism and Buddhism. Asoka was born

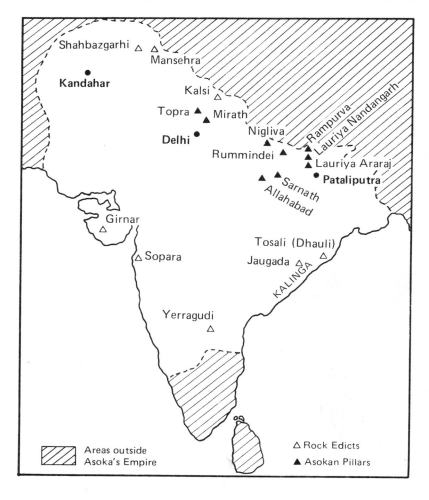

Areas outside Asoka's Empire
△ Rock Edicts
▲ Asokan Pillars

Hindu, but was converted to Buddhism. His rule therefore gives us the chance to examine these two great religions, which we shall do in the second part of this booklet. There we shall also consider the working of the great social system of Hindu India — the caste system.

CHANDRAGUPTA AND THE FOUNDING OF THE MAURYAN EMPIRE

In another booklet *(Alexander)** you can read about Alexander the Great, the ruler of Greece, whose armies marched through the Middle East and into northern India (D1).** In India, Alexander met Chandragupta, a young man who was not afraid of voicing his opinions. Alexander responded by giving orders for his capture. However, Chandragupta managed to escape and take refuge in a forest in central India. Here he met a Brahmin who had quarrelled with the ruler of Magadha, the greatest Hindu kingdom in northern India. Chandragupta agreed to help the Brahmin in his search for revenge by leading an army against Magadha, and in 321 BC he seized the capital city — Pataliputra (modern Patna in Bihar). By 313 BC he had conquered central and western India, and his kingdom, the Mauryan Empire, extended from Patna in the east to the Indus River in the west. This was the eastern border of the Greek Empire, which was no longer strong enough to resist attacks by Chandragupta's army. The Greeks agreed to give Afghanistan and Baluchistan to the Mauryan king, in return for 55 war elephants. Chandragupta then married a Greek general's daughter and the Greeks appointed an envoy to the court at Pataliputra.

BINDUSARA

Bindusara, Chandragupta's son, came to the throne after his father's death in about 302 BC. He was not warlike, so he did not extend the Empire of Magadha during his reign, although he proved himself able to hold together what he had inherited. Friendly relations with the Greek Empire continued. Bindusara's reign of about 29 years was a period of peace and stability for his kingdom, a period which was shattered by the fierce war of succession fought by his three sons after his death in 273 BC.

ASOKA

Asoka, Bindusara's second son, who was successful in winning the throne of Magadha, was quite unlike his father. He began to expand his empire with the aim of establishing his rule over eastern and parts of southern India. Such imperial expansion resulted in constant warfare and bloodshed for eight stormy years.

Then came the great turning-point in Asoka's life, his campaign against Kalinga, or Orissa, in eastern India. Kalinga was conquered, but resistance was so fierce that 150,000 people were carried off as prisoners, 100,000

* Titles in brackets refer to other booklets in the Program

** The reference (D) indicates the numbered documents at the end of this book.

no longer would he rely on force of arms, but on the power of righteousness, or *dharma*, to maintain his empire and his own position within it. Thus the deadly Kalinga campaign produced results of far-reaching consequence in the history of India and the whole eastern world.

Like most of his people Asoka was a Hindu; but his change of heart caused him to turn to the teachings of Gautama, the Buddha. Born about 130 years before, the Buddha had attempted to change

The lion-carving at the head of the most famous of Asokan pillars at Sarnath, near Benares. The quality of the carving on this pillar is said to be the finest in the whole of the ancient world

The bull-carving which crowns the Asokan pillar put up at Rampurva, northern Bihar

were killed in battle, and many others died as a result of the hardships and atrocities of war.

Such scenes of bloodshed so horrified the young emperor (D2) that soon after the Kalinga campaign he gave up warfare, and sent peace missions all over India, and even to such distant places as Burma and Sumatra. His whole attitude to conquest changed:

4

the more oppressive aspects of Hinduism, and had ended by establishing his own religion —Buddhism — now the fourth largest in the world.

Government

Asoka worked for and established an all-India empire, something which had never been achieved before. The country was ruled with the help of an efficient civil service, good roads and a strong army.

To maintain an army strong enough to protect his vast empire, Asoka needed a large and regular income. Since the majority of people earned a living from agriculture, the chief source of this income was a tax on land. Officers were appointed to supervize the collection of taxes at both district and village level, and special inspectors were sent out to spread Asoka's word to the people and bring back their complaints. Many spies kept Asoka informed of what was going on in his kingdom.

Asoka established hospitals and good roads with resthouses throughout his kingdom (D3). The longest road, measuring about 1000 miles, ran all the way from Pataliputra to Afghanistan. In exchange for food and shelter the poorest people in society were employed to work on government projects. These included the turning of waste ground into good agricultural land by drainage or irrigation, and the working of mines in the Punjab and Bihar.

Military Organization

Chandragupta's army numbered 9000 elephants, 30,000 cavalry and 600,000 infantry. After Asoka had renounced war, this force was probably reduced, but he maintained high salaries for his officers to encourage them to work well.

Guilds

The new and good roads improved trade, both within the country and overseas. This led to an increase in the profits of the trade guilds. The merchants and craftsmen who belonged to these guilds became wealthy, and special rules were made to control the strength of the guilds.

Asoka's Dharma

The emperor Asoka became a follower of the teaching of Buddha. At the same time he put forward his own doctrine of *dharma*. Throughout his empire he erected inscribed pillars, ten of which still stand, in order to encourage both the spread of Buddhism and the observance of his *dharma*. Asoka's *dharma* was based on toleration and non-violence, with the aim of preserving the social order. His teachings were very like those of Christianity. They stressed toleration, non-violence, respect for those in positions of authority, including Brahmins and Buddhist monks (D4), and consideration and kindness towards inferiors

(D5). In its content his *dharma* was not new; what was original was the way he used this code to unite his people and hold them together, giving India a period of peace and good government.

Village Life and Agriculture

There were three types of landowner: those who worked their own land; those who leased their land, receiving rent in the form of half the annual crop; and those who employed labourers. The last group included the emperor and the temples, most of which owned large estates.

The majority of people owned farms which were barely large enough to support a family. To make the best use of their limited possessions men sometimes worked their land jointly, sharing tools and work animals. Family wealth was estimated by the number of animals owned: cows and buffaloes, sheep and goats and sometimes pigs. Cattle from the village were sent out to graze every day in the charge of a cowherd.

There were three annual crops, of which the most important was rice (D6). Wheat and barley were also grown, and vegetables such as peas, beans and lentils. Flax and hemp were cultivated, as well as sugar cane (D7). Near the villages were orchards which produced a surplus of fruit for sale in nearby towns (D8).

Asoka's 40-feet-high lion column at Lauriya-Nandangarh. Asoka's inscriptions can still be seen on this pillar of polished sandstone

6

The individual peasant farmer was heavily taxed. He also had to contribute to the tax which the government collected from each village and to special taxes for services provided by the government. These included the building of extensive and complicated irrigation systems consisting of canals, wells and reservoirs; and protection against theft etc. The state encouraged farmers to cultivate new land by providing cash advances and the loan of tools, and a farmer who did this was considered owner of the land after five years.

Many popular Hindu festivals arose as celebrations of the annual seasons which could have an all-important effect on the prosperity and fertility of crops and herds. Such festivals provided almost the only break from the monotonous round of daily work in the villages.

Like the towns, the villages were surrounded by protective walls, and entered by large gateways which were closed at night. Houses were simpler and smaller than those of the cities, and made of readily-available local materials; shops resembled market-stalls, and customers mingled freely with wandering cattle as they made their purchases. Often there would be a sacred tree at which the village-women would make daily offerings, for religious belief was strong among the country-folk.

City and Court Life

Northern India at the time of Asoka had many wealthy cities.

An artist's impression of a typical city of the Asokan period – perhaps Pataliputra, the Asokan capital

The capital of the Mauryan empire, Pataliputra, twenty-five miles in perimeter, was the greatest. Towns were fortified by walls of huge tree-trunks sunk into the ground. Watch-towers were built at intervals round these battlements, and there were large guarded gateways in each wall of the town where the toll-collectors had their offices. Bridges were built up to these gateways, over the moats which surrounded the town. A never-ending stream of traffic went in and out of the town all day: men, women and children coming from the countryside with vegetables and fruit for sale in the markets; elephants carrying high-ranking nobles; merchants arriving with loaded caravans, bearing gold, ivory, jewels, rich materials and slaves; pilgrims and troops of cavalry. At nightfall, the heavy wooden doors, strengthened with great iron bars, which served as a defence for the city at night, were closed. At midnight, a curfew was imposed. Only spies and those on urgent, secret, official business moved about after this, using the specially constructed tunnels and passage-ways leading from the centre of the city to distant parts of the countryside, to make their getaway speedy and secure. Outside the city, poor and often slummy suburbs developed around slaughter-houses, execution areas and cemeteries. The busy streets of the town were cobbled, and were wide enough for the carriages of the nobles.

At the centre of the city, at the end of the largest and grandest of the roads, stood the royal palace, overlooking the best residential areas, full of detached houses often several storeys high, with gardens and courtyards containing attractive pools. Here, too, were found hospitals, maternity homes, homes for aged or sick animals, alms-houses for the relief of beggars and the poor, rest-houses for travellers, and educational institutions where scholars lived. There were also many parks and pleasure-gardens.

Public art galleries, the musicians' quarters, and the main administrative offices of the city were to be found near the palace, which was almost a small city in itself. Like the town in which it was situated, it was surrounded by battlements fortified by heavily-guarded watch-towers. The palace was divided into two sections: first was the public area, open to all, housing the King's granaries, almshouses, stables and art galleries. The area also contained pavilions and gardens in which royal audiences were held, or plays and concerts performed. Second was the private area, containing the monarch's own dwelling and that of his women, the harem. In this area, too, were the chief official departments of the kingdom, such as the armoury and the treasury.

The harem was a place of extreme luxury and equally extreme monotony. The king, while having one official wife, was also allowed many concubines. The harem was like a beauty salon, and specialist servants were employed for each task: the making of ointments and perfumes; the dressing of the hair;

massage; the preparation of incense for the women's private rooms and to perfume their garments; and the use of make-up. The women amused themselves listening to music; watching dancers and acrobats; walking in the extensive parks; choosing cosmetics, perfumes and clothes; playing with pet animals and birds; or swimming and bathing in the numerous pools within the harem grounds.

The king's day was busy and largely taken up by government affairs (D9). He rose before dawn, to be immediately faced with urgent political matters needing attention. He held a daily council with his ministers of state, then would greet members of his family and household. Afterwards

Brahma, the Supreme Spirit worshipped by Hindus. He represents the creative aspect of the Hindu Trinity of Brahma, Vishnu and Shiva

he would hold a public audience, receiving reports from his regional administrators, and hearing individual requests and complaints from his subjects.

After lunch and a rest, the king would again see his ministers, tax-inspectors and Treasury officials, and his informants who had returned from distant parts of the kingdom (D10). After this he was free to enjoy himself with painting, poetry and music; archery; chess or dice-playing; cock-fighting; and inspecting his horses and elephants. In the evening his spies would come to report; indeed, it was a rule that affairs of state must always take precedence over pleasure, so that the king would often have to break his siesta for more urgent and pressing business.

The Hindu God Vishnu, protector of the universe. It is believed that when good forces are threatened, he reincarnates himself in various forms to punish wrongdoers, uphold the righteous and re-establish dharma

A king like Asoka, with a highly developed sense of duty and responsibility, would have little time for relaxation and amusement (D11). *(The Growth of the State).*

HINDUISM

When Asoka came to power, Hinduism was the dominant religion in India, as it still is today. Hinduism, of course, has altered through the centuries. By the time of Asoka there were three main gods: Brahma the creator, Vishnu the preserver, and Shiva the destroyer. Vishnu is the god who, whenever the world or mankind is in danger, is born again to overcome whatever evil threatens. Shiva, although termed the 'destroyer', is better thought of as a 'regenerator' : just as plants will only grow if others decay, so all things may only be renewed through initial

Shiva, third aspect of the Hindu Trinity, who maintains the cycle of existence by destroying material things and beings so that regeneration may take place

11

Aryans — ancestors of the present-day Indians — absorbed into their own faith many basic values of the people they conquered, most notably, perhaps, the belief in a mother-goddess. Of course they also brought their own gods and social system to India. In this traditional Hindu social system there were four main classes *(varna)* (D13).

The Brahmins

To secure the goodwill and protection of the gods, the chiefs and wealthy men of the Aryan tribes provided many animals for mass sacrifice. The ceremony was performed by religious specialists, or priests, according to complicated rules: any mistakes would make the gods angry. The importance of the priests is obvious. Only they knew the sacred texts; only they could correctly perform sacrifice. One mistake by a priest might result in national disaster. The priests were said to possess a magical power, or *brahman,* and ultimately the priests themselves became known as Brahmans, or Brahmins. *(Religion)*

The Brahmins were the highest of the four *varna*, and all other men owed them respect. They were often given goods, money or land, and so became owners of large estates, which were cultivated for them by labourers or slaves. Brahmins did not pay any taxes and were exempt from many legal penalties. A crime against one of them was severely punished.

Many Brahmins were writers and religious scholars, school-masters or university teachers, advisers to the king or administrators. Some, however, exploited their privileged position, becoming arrogant and oppressive. People lost their respect for the whole class which, under Buddhism, suffered a decline in status. Deprived of their traditional support from gifts, some Brahmins took up new jobs as tax collectors, army officers, spies, servants, or hired labourers. Nevertheless intelligent Brahmins, and those with a truly devout way of life, continued to act as advisers at court and as royal priests, even to Buddhist kings like Asoka himself.

The Kshatriyas

This *varna*, ranking second in the social hierarchy, consisted of warriors and the ruling aristocracy, including the royal family. Their education included training in warfare and use of arms. They were also employed as provincial governors, administrators and royal representatives. The Brahmins relied upon the Kshatriyas for gifts and protection, while the Kshatriyas would have been unable to govern without the assistance of their Brahmin advisers and administrators.

The Vaishyas

The Vaishyas ranked third, some way below the Brahmins and Kshatriyas. They were engaged in agriculture (sometimes as peasant farmers, sometimes as rich landowners), or trade (either as traded in — precious metals and jewels; cloth; perfumes; spices, etc. — and these guilds were very powerful within the state. Occasionally, the ruler would choose an adviser from this *varna*. Vaishyas paid higher taxes than others — thus they carried out their traditional role of working for and maintaining the two higher *varna*.

The Shudras

This group, the lowest of the four *varna*, was probably first composed of the darker-skinned original inhabitants of northern India, conquered by the Aryans and forced to undertake humble tasks. Some poor or disgraced Aryans may have been absorbed into this class in time. The ·Shudras had few rights, the main ones being protection under the law, and the privilege of learning certain specific texts of the Hindu scriptures. They had, however, many duties, their job being to serve the three higher *varna* conscientiously and unquestioningly. The class was mainly composed of petty traders, artisans, agricultural labourers, unskilled workers, and craftsmen. Each workman, with his family, was generally attached to a particular wealthy landowner or other rich men, who saw to it that the man and his dependants were fed, clothed and given a place to live in return for work done. An employer was also supposed to give his workmen tools suitable for the job they had to do. If he forced his employees to work longer hours than those agreed

Durga, fierce aspect of the goddess Parvati, Shiva's consort (wife), seen here destroying the devil in half-man, half-buffalo form. She is a later development within Hinduism of the mother goddess of pre-Aryan India

small shopkeepers, or as wealthy merchants with international trading partners in Europe, China, the Middle East and Africa). They organized powerful trade guilds, according to the goods which they and did not provide adequate food and shelter, he could be prosecuted under the law. Thus the Shudras, though condemned to dirty, low-paid jobs, were safeguarded to some extent. This *varna* was divided into 'clean' and 'unclean' categories. Those with particularly dirty jobs, such as the leather-workers, brewers, or butchers, would pollute (that is, make dirty and unfit to mix with others) members of the higher *varna* by their touch, or even by their approach, hence the origin of the term 'untouchable'. Those who were polluted would have to undergo ritual purification.

The Hindu God Ganesha, son of Shiva and Parvati, who is invoked at the beginning of all rituals except funerals. Legend tells how Shiva, in a fit of anger, chopped off his son's head, which he then, in remorse, replaced with that of an elephant

The Caste System

These four *varna* provided the framework for the caste system. Each *varna* consisted of many castes, which were further sub-divided into sub-castes. Marriage was generally not allowed to take place between members of different castes, particularly if they belonged to different *varna*. Although the coming of Buddhism reduced the privileges of the highest *varna* for some time, it did not do away with the caste system altogether.

The caste system was justified by the Hindu doctrine of rebirth. The soul of every living creature was re-born higher or lower in the social scale according to how well the duties of life had been performed in an earlier existence. Thus a Brahmin was being rewarded for the fine quality of his previous life on earth, while the sweeper or butcher was justly suffering for his past failure.

To ensure a happier state of affairs in his next existence, a man had to perform his duty within that sphere of life to which he was born. This caste duty was called *dharma,* and it was said that it was better to do one's own caste duty badly than another's well (D14).

Slavery

In addition to the four main classes there were also slaves in the Mauryan empire. As slaves were cheap, slave-owning was fairly widespread. In the Royal Palace lived foreign girls, many of them Greek, supposedly skilled in music and the arts, who were brought by traders for the royal harem; the guardians of the harem, too, were members of an armed force of women, who would also accompany the emperor on his hunting expeditions (D15,16), and guard him (D17).

The working conditions of the slaves varied. Some were allowed to earn money in their spare time (if they had any), with which they could buy their freedom. It was a rule that every slave was allowed at least one opportunity to escape; if he was able to avoid his pursuers, he was then regarded as a free man.

Some people became slaves through personal misfortune; for instance, a debtor could work off what he owed by becoming the slave of his creditor for a limited period. Criminals could be sentenced to a term of slavery; prisoners of war were enslaved, usually for the period of one year only.

In one respect slaves were better off than members of the Shudra castes, since they were sure of being cared for if sick or old.

BUDDHISM

Gautama, the Buddha, was born about 480 BC in the foothills of the Himalayas, the son of a chieftain, and a Kshatriya by caste. His birth had been foretold to his mother in a dream; it was said that he was destined to become either a Universal Emperor or a Universal Teacher. Gautama's father was determined that his son would become a great ruler, and did his best to ensure that he would not become a Universal Teacher. Gautama's days were made as happy as possible; all evil was kept from him, lest he should feel the need to work to improve the lot of mankind.

Nevertheless, in spite of his father's efforts, Gautama saw four signs which convinced him of the misery of the world: a very old man, in the last stages of weakness; a desperately sick man,

The Lord Buddha preaching his first sermon to his disciples in the Deer Park near Benares after becoming Buddha – the 'Enlightened One'

suffering from fever; and a corpse, being carried to cremation, followed by the sorrowing relatives. The fourth sign was more hopeful: a wandering religious man, poor, begging for his food, wearing only a plain yellow robe, but nevertheless filled with inner joy. Gautama determined that he would follow the example of this monk, but his father would have none of it, and kept him virtually a prisoner until the birth of Gautama's first son. In the middle of the festivities the prince seized his opportunity and rode away into the night.

At first Gautama became a wandering beggar, then a forest hermit. He starved himself until he was almost dead; but this, still, brought him no nearer the answer to his problem. He vowed that he would sit beneath a pipal tree and think until the mystery of suffering was revealed to him; and there he sat for forty-nine days, enduring great temptations, hardships and suffering until he finally understood the nature of suffering and unhappiness and what man must do to overcome them.

Gautama, now called the Buddha, began his life's work of teaching, preaching and prayer, and gathered a group of disciples, who wore yellow robes, and lived in poverty (D18) according to certain rules of life. The Buddha's holy life, his wisdom, and his miraculous acts brought him a wide following, even among the ruling class. To him bloodshed, whether human or animal, was evil and useless; it was violence, and to

The Nirvana of Buddha. He is shown surrounded by his followers as his soul passes from earthly life to union with the Supreme Spirit

commit violence was to disrupt the peaceful order of things and bring disharmony into the world (D19,20).

Buddha's ministry was long and peaceful; he died at the age of eighty, back in the foothills of places, and after his death he was worshipped at sacred pipal trees, reminders of his long meditation and enlightenment, and *stupas*, symbols of his death. These were built all over India and beyond, as his teaching, with the

The Great Stupa, or Buddhist shrine, at Sanchi in central India. The original building on this site was erected by Asoka

the Himalayas, the home of his youth (D21). His body was cremated, and his ashes were subsequently divided among various shrines, called *stupas,* all over India; Asoka himself built many of these shrines.

Two hundred years aftèr Buddha's death his teaching had been recognized as a distinct religion, and in Asoka's time many Buddhist monasteries, each with its own temple, were established (D22). Buddha had always encouraged his followers to respect local shrines and holy encouragement of Asoka, spread overseas. The great Buddhist holy places became centres of pilgrimage, and the Emperor Asoka himself payed homage to the Universal Teacher at these centres.

As Buddhism spread, not only throughout India but also to Sri Lanka and south-east Asia the ideals of the Buddha became a living faith to thousands of ordinary men and women. In practice these ideals emphasized the desirability of living in peace with one's fellow-men; the value

and sacredness of life, both human and animal; tolerance of the beliefs and customs of others, and a consequent humility; and the equality of all men in the sight of God.

So seriously did Asoka view the Buddhist doctrine regarding the sanctity of all life, that he encouraged the spread of vegetarianism throughout his kingdom, and insisted that no animal be slain for food for the royal palace (D23). Buddhists, like Hindus, believed in rebirth, and since a man's soul might pass to an animal in his next existence, all living things, even the meanest insects, should be treated with consideration.

ASOKA AND INDIAN CIVILIZATION IN WORLD HISTORY

Asoka was the first to build an empire which covered most of India. Although it broke up after his death future rulers of India tried to rebuild an all-Indian empire. Asoka also introduced a new style of government based upon morality, not force. Of course, most rulers prefer people to obey them willingly than to have the trouble of forcing them to obey, but Asoka was one of the first to fit the ideals of toleration and non-violence into his system of government. These ideals played an important part in later Indian and world history. *(Gandhi)*

Asoka also helped to establish the Buddhist religion. Although Buddhism gradually declined in India after his death, and by AD 1300, after the Muslim invasions, *(Akbar and the Mughal Empire)* had virtually disappeared from that country, it was partly due to Asoka that Buddhism became established in east and south-east Asia where it is still so important.

Finally, Asoka's career shows us how little impact even a great traditional ruler could have upon a strong social system such as that of Hinduism. Indian village life was not changed by Asoka's rule. The Hindu social system in fact was strengthened by his attacks upon it, and the power of the higher castes became greater. Until modern times the pattern of people's lives was determined by the land, the rivers, the climate and the caste system. Only under the impact of the great revolutions of the modern world has Hindu life changed.

A close-up of the East Gate of the Great Stupa at Sanchi. The fine sculpture, still clear after 2300 years, show scenes of the daily life of the period

DOCUMENT 1

ALEXANDER AND THE BRAHMINS   *ARISTOBOULOS POTIDAEA*
— One of Alexander's officers, in India in 326 BC

Aristoboulos says that in Taxila he saw two of the sages, both Brahmins;
the elder had his head shaved, but the other wore his hair; both of them
were followed by their disciples. Their spare time is spent in the market-
place; in respect of their being public counsellors they receive great
homage, and have the privilege of taking without payment whatever they
want that is offered for sale; on every person whom they greet they pour
oil of sesamum until it trickles down to their face; of honey, which is
exposed for sale in great quantity, and of sesamum they take enough to
make cakes, and their food costs them nothing. They came to
Alexander's table and took their meal standing, and gave an example of
their endurance by retiring to a place that was near where the elder lying
on his back endured the sun and the rains which were now falling, as
spring had by this time set in. The other stood on one leg holding up
with both his hands a beam of wood; when the leg became fatigued he
supported himself on the other, and continued thus the whole day long.
The younger seemed to have far greater self-control, for having followed
the king for a short distance he quickly turned back home. The king sent
after him, but he requested the king to come to him if he wanted
anything at his hands. The other accompanied the king to the end of his
days, and in staying with him dressed in a different style and altered his
whole mode of life.

DOCUMENT 2

THE CONQUEST OF KALINGA   *ASOKA — An extract from one of*
his inscriptions

Kalinga was conquered by the King when he had been consecrated eight
years. One hundred and fifty thousand persons were thence carried away
captive, one hundred thousand were there slain, and many times that
number died.

   Directly after the Kalingas had been annexed began His Sacred
Majesty's zealous protection of the Law of Piety, his love of that Law,
and his inculcation of the Law. Thence arises the King's sorrow for having
conquered the Kalingas, because the conquest of a country previously
unconquered involves the slaughter, death, and carrying away captive
of the people. That is a matter of profound sorrow and regret to His
Sacred Majesty.

   So that of all the people who were then slain, done to death, or
carried away captive in Kalinga, if the hundredth part or the thousandth
part were now to suffer the same fate, it would be a matter of regret to
His Sacred Majesty.

DOCUMENT 3

HELP FOR TRAVELLERS   *ASOKA*

On the roads I have had banyan-trees planted to give shade to man and beast; groves of mango-trees I have had planted; at intervals I have had wells dug; rest-houses, too, have been erected; and numerous watering-places have been provided by me here and there for the enjoyment of man and beast.

DOCUMENT 4

INTERCASTE DUTIES   *DIGHA NIKAYA — Buddhist scripture*
written about 300 BC

In five ways a gentleman should serve ascetics and Brahmins: by affectionate acts; by affectionate words; by affectionate thoughts; by not closing his doors to them; and by duly supplying them with food. Thus served by a gentleman they should care for him in six ways: they should feel for him with a friendly mind; they should teach him what he has not heard before; they should encourage him to follow what he has already learned; and they should show him the way to heaven.

DOCUMENT 5

TOLERATION   *ASOKA*

The King honours men of all sects, whether ascetics or householders, by gifts and various forms of reverence.

However, the King cares not so much for gifts or external reverence as that there should be a growth of the essence of Dharma in all sects . . . the root of it is restraint of speech, that is, a man must not honour his own sect or disparage that of another without reason. Depreciation should be for specific reasons only, because the sects of other people all deserve reverence for one reason or another.

DOCUMENT 6

DAILY LIFE AND CUSTOMS   *MEGASTHENES — Greek ambassador*
to the Mauryan kingdom from about 302 to 300 BC

Indians lead happy lives, being simple in their manners and frugal. They never drink wine except at sacrifices. Their beverage is prepared from rice instead of barley, and their food is principally rice. The simplicity of their laws and their contracts appears from the fact that they seldom go to law. Their houses and property are for the most part unguarded. These things show their moderation and good sense, but other things they do which one cannot approve — that they always eat alone, and that they have no fixed hours when all take their meals in common, but each one eats when it pleases himself. The contrary custom would be better for the interests of social and political life.

DOCUMENT 7

THE INDIANS AND THEIR COUNTRY   *STRABO — A Greek historian born about 63 BC*

During the rainy season flax and millet, as well as sesamum, rice, and bosmoron are sown; and in the winter season, wheat, barley, pulse, and other esculents with which we are unacquainted. Nearly the same animals are bred in India as in Ethiopia and in Egypt, and the Indian rivers produce all the animals found in the rivers of these countries, except the hippopotamus. With regard to the inhabitants, the men of the south resemble the Ethiopians in their complexion, but in their face and in their hair they are like other people; for their hair does not curl on account of the moistness of the atmosphere. The men of the north again are like the Egyptians.

DOCUMENT 8

FARMING AND FARMERS   *MEGASTHENES*

It is said that famine has never visited India, and that there has never been a general scarcity in the supply of nourishing food. For, since there is a double rainfall in the course of each year — one in the winter season, when the sowing of wheat takes place as in other countries, and the second in summer — the inhabitants of India almost always gather in two harvests annually . . . . The wild fruits, as well, and the esculent roots which grow in marshy places and are of varied sweetness, afford abundant food for man. The fact is, almost all the plains in the country are well-watered, whether from the rivers, or from the rains of the summer season, which fall every year at a stated period with surprising regularity; while the great heat which prevails ripens the roots which grow in marshes, and especially those of the tall reeds.

But, further, there are customs observed by the Indians which help to prevent famine; for while among other nations it is usual, in war, to lay waste the soil, and thus to reduce it to an uncultivated waste, among the Indians, on the contrary, by whom farmers are regarded as a class that is sacred and inviolable, the tillers of the soil, even when battle is raging in their neighbourhood, are undisturbed by any sense of danger, for the soldiers on either side in waging war kill each other, but allow those engaged in farming to remain quite unharmed.

DOCUMENT 9

KING AND SUBJECTS   *KAUTILIYA — Chandragupta's Prime Minister and close friend.*

Only if a king is himself energetically active, do his officers follow him energetically. If he is sluggish, they too remain sluggish. And, besides, they eat up his works. He is thereby easily overpowered by his enemies.

In the happiness of the subjects lies the happiness of the king; in their welfare, his own welfare. The welfare of the king does not lie in the fulfillment of what is dear to him; whatever is dear to the subjects constitutes his welfare.

DOCUMENT 10

THE KNOWLEDGE OF ECONOMICS   *KAUTILIYA*

Agriculture, cattle-breeding, trade, and commerce constitute the main topics dealt with in the science of economics; it is helpful on account of its making available grains, cattle, gold, raw materials, and free labour. Through the knowledge of economics, a king brings under his control his own party and the enemy's party with the help of treasury and army.

DOCUMENT 11

THE PRINCIPLES OF GOVERNMENT   *ASOKA*

The King said:
When I have been consecrated twenty-six years I caused the Law of Piety to be written.

Both this world and the next are difficult to secure except by intense love of the Law of Piety, complete self-examination, complete obedience, complete dread, complete effort. However, owing to my instruction, this longing for the Law of Piety, this love of the Law from day to day, have grown and will grow.

My Agents, too, whether of high, low, or middle rank, themselves follow my teaching and lead others in the right way (fickle people must be led in the right way), likewise also the Lords of the Borderlands. For this is the rule: 'protection by the Law of Piety, regulation by that Law, happiness by that Law, guarding by that Law'.

DOCUMENT 12

RELEASE FROM REBIRTH   *THE UPANISHADS — Hindu scriptures*
written about 600 BC

Those who practice penance and faith in the forest, the tranquil ones, the knowers of truth, living the life of wandering mendicancy (begging) — they depart, freed from passion, through the door of the sun, to where dwells, verily, that immortal Purusha, the imperishable Soul.

DOCUMENT 13

THE ORIGIN OF CASTE   *RIG VEDA — Oldest of the Hindu scriptures*

When they divided Purusha, in how many different portions did they arrange him? What became of his mouth, what of his two arms? What were his two thighs and his two feet called?

His mouth became the Brahman; his two arms were made into the Rajanya; his two thighs the Vaishyas; from his two feet the Shudra was born.

DOCUMENT 14

THE WAY TO HEAVEN   *DIGHA NIKAYA*

A Kshatriya who has led a bad life, whether in deed, word, or thought,

26

and who has had wrong views about the world, because of his outlook and his deeds will be reborn after parting with his body in the waste and woeful pit of purgatory. And a Brahman, a Vaishya, and a Shudra will fare likewise. If on the other hand they lead good lives in thought, word and deed, and have right views about the world, they will be reborn in the happy world of heaven. If their lives and their views are mixed they will be reborn in a state where they feel both happiness and sorrow. But if they are self-restrained in body, speech and mind . . . they may find Nirvana, even in this present life.

DOCUMENT 15

ELEPHANT-HUNTING   *MEGASTHENES*

Round a bare piece of ground is dug a deep ditch, and over this a very narrow bridge is thrown at the place of entrance. Into the enclosure three or four of the tamest female elephants are then driven. Then men themselves lie in wait in concealed huts. The wild elephants do not approach this trap by day, but they enter it by night in single file. When all have passed the entrance, the men secretly close it. They then introduce the strongest of the tame combatants, the drivers of which fight with the wild animals, and also exhaust them by hunger. When the latter are at length tired, the boldest of the drivers dismount unobserved, and each of them creeps under his own elephant, and from there gets under the wild elephant and ties his legs together. When this has been done they make the tame elephants beat those which are tied by the legs till they fall to the ground. Thereupon they bind the wild and tame elephants together by the neck with thongs of raw ox-hide. From the number taken, those that are too old or too young to be useful are rejected, and the rest are led away to the stables. In the next place they teach them to obey, effecting this by soothing them, some by words, and others by song and the music of the drum. Few of them are difficult to be tamed, for they are naturally of a mild and gentle disposition. Some of them have taken up their drivers who have fallen in battle and carried them off safely from the field. Others have fought in defence of their masters who had sought refuge by creeping between their forelegs, and have thus saved their lives. If in a fit of anger they kill either the man who feeds them or the man who trains them, they are so overpowered with regret that they refuse food, and sometimes die of hunger.

DOCUMENT 16

MONKEY-HUNTING   *STRABO*

The chase of this animal is conducted in two ways. It is an imitative
creature, and takes refuge up in trees. The hunters, when they see it
sitting on a tree, set down in its sight a basin containing water with
which they wash their own eyes; then they set down a basin full of
bird-lime instead of water, go away, and lie in wait some distance off.
The ape now leaps down and smears its eyes with the bird-lime, and
when it can no longer see, the hunters come up and capture it alive. This
is one method, and the other is as follows. The hunters, having dressed
themselves in bags like trousers, go off and hide themselves, leaving
other bags behind them of a rough, shaggy texture, smeared over inside
with bird-lime. Then the apes get inside these and are easily captured.

DOCUMENT 17

A KING'S LIFE   *MEGASTHENES*

The care of the king's person is entrusted to women, who are bought
from their parents. The king leaves his palace not only in time of war,
but when he has to sit in the law-court. He remains there for the whole
day without allowing the business to be interrupted. Another purpose
for which he leaves his palace is to offer sacrifice; a third is to go
hunting. Crowds of women surround him, and on the outside are
spearmen. The road is marked off with ropes, and it is death for a man or
even for a woman to pass within the ropes. Men with drums and gongs
lead the procession. The king hunts in the enclosures and shoots arrows
from a platform. At his side stand two or three armed women. If he
hunts in the open grounds, he shoots from the back of an elephant. Of
the women, some ride in chariots, some on horses, and some even on
elephants, and they are equipped with all sorts of weapons, as if they
were going on a military expedition.

DOCUMENT 18

TREASURE WHICH NO ONE CAN STEAL   *KHUDDAKA PATHA*
 — *Early Buddhist scripture written about 300 BC*

Treasure may not profit the owner at all, for he may forget where he has

28

hidden it, or goblins may steal it, or his enemies or even his kinsmen may take it when he is careless.

But by charity, goodness, restraint, and self-control man and woman alike can store up a well-hidden treasure — a treasure which cannot be given to others and which robbers cannot steal. A wise man should do good — that is the treasure which will not leave him.

DOCUMENT 19

LOVE OVERCOMES HATRED   *DHAMMAPADA — An ancient Buddhist poem.*

> Never in this world is hate
>   Appeased by hatred;
> It is only appeased by love —
>   This is an eternal law.
>
> Victory breeds hatred
>   For the defeated lie down in sorrow.
> Above victory or defeat
>   The calm man dwells in peace.

DOCUMENT 20

THE VIRTUE OF FRIENDLINESS   *SUTTA NIPATA — A collection of Buddhist teachings containing many of the oldest pieces of poetry*

> As a mother cares for her son,
> Her only son, all her days,
> So towards all things living
> A man's mind should be all-embracing.
> Friendliness for the whole world,
> All-embracing, he should raise in his mind,
> Above, below, and across,
> Unhindered, free from hate and ill-will.

DOCUMENT 21

BUDDHA IN HEAVEN   *MILINDAPANHA — An early Buddhist text*
written about 130 BC

'Reverend Nagasena', said the King, 'does the Buddha still exist?'
'Yes, your Majesty, he does.'
'Then it is possible to point out the Buddha as being here or there?'
'The Lord has passed completely away in Nirvana, so that nothing is left
which could lead to the formation of another being. And so he cannot be
pointed out as being here or there. If a great fire were blazing, would it
be possible to point to a flame which had gone out and say that it was
here or there?'
'No, your Reverence, the flame is extinguished, it can't be detected.'
'In just the same way, your Majesty, the Lord has passed away in
Nirvana . . . . He can only be pointed out in the body of his doctrine, for
it was he who taught it.'

DOCUMENT 22

BUDDHIST PHILOSOPHERS (THE PRAMNAI)   *STRABO*

The Pramnai are philosophers opposed to the Brahmins, and are very
argumentative. They ridicule the Brahmins who study physiology and
astronomy as fools and imposters.

The Pramnai of the city live in towns and wear muslin robes, while
those of the country wear the skins of fawns or antelopes. In a word, the
Indians wear white — white muslin or linen; all of them wear long hair
and long beards, plait their hair and bind it.

DOCUMENT 23

THE SACREDNESS OF LIFE   *ASOKA — One of his Rock Edicts*

Here no animal may be slaughtered for sacrifice, nor shall any merry-
making be held. Because in merry-makings the King sees much offence,
although certain merry-makings are excellent in his sight. Formerly, in
the King's kitchen each day many hundred thousands of living creatures
were slaughtered to make curries. But now, when this scripture of the
Law is being written, only three living creatures are slaughtered for curry
daily, two peacocks and one antelope — the antelope, however, not
always. Even those three living creatures shall not be slaughtered in
future.

ACKNOWLEDGMENTS

British Museum pages 9, 10, 11, 14, 15; Government of India (by permission of Arthur Probsthain) page 12; India Office Library page 4 (left); *Indian Architecture*, Percy Brown, D.B. Taraporevala Sons page 7.

Greenhaven World History Program

History Makers
Alexander
Constantine
Leonardo Da Vinci
Columbus
Luther, Erasmus and Loyola
Napoleon
Bolivar
Adam Smith, Malthus and Marx
Darwin
Bismark
Henry Ford
Roosevelt
Stalin
Mao Tse-Tung
Gandhi
Nyerere and Nkrumah

Great Civilizations
The Ancient Near East
Ancient Greece
Pax Romana
The Middle Ages
Spices and Civilization
Chingis Khan and the Mongol Empire
Akbar and the Mughal Empire
Traditional China
Ancient America
Traditional Africa
Asoka and Indian Civilization
Mohammad and the Arab Empire
Ibin Sina and the Muslim World
Suleyman and the Ottoman Empire

Great Revolutions
The Neolithic Revolution
The Agricultural Revolution
The Scientific Revolution
The Industrial Revolution
The Communications Revolution
The American Revolution
The French Revolution
The Mexican Revolution
The Russian Revolution
The Chinese Revolution

Enduring Issues
Cities
Population
Health and Wealth
A World Economy
Law
Religion
Language
Education
The Family

Political and Social Movements
The Slave Trade
The Enlightenment
Imperialism
Nationalism
The British Raj and Indian Nationalism
The Growth of the State
The Suez Canal
The American Frontier
Japan's Modernization
Hitler's Reich
The Two World Wars
The Atom Bomb
The Cold War
The Wealth of Japan
Hollywood